CW01112318

Ntailan Lolkoki is an activist against female genital mutilation who has so far published her autobiography narrating her life through FGM. Ntailan also published a second book with Austin Macauley, a novel called *The Kingdom of Watetu and Songaland,* using her life and the lives of other victims to educate on the subject. She is also a public speaker who encourages young people to say no to female genital mutilation and other forms of abuse.

Life After Reconstruction

Ntailan Lolkoki

Austin Macauley Publishers™
LONDON • CAMBRIDGE • NEW YORK • SHARJAH

Copyright © Ntailan Lolkoki 2023

The right of **Ntailan Lolkoki** to be identified as author of this work has been asserted by the author in accordance with sections 77 and 78 of the Copyright, Designs and Patents Act 1988.

All rights reserved. No part of this publication may be reproduced, stored in a retrieval system, or transmitted in any form or by any means, electronic, mechanical, photocopying, recording, or otherwise, without the prior permission of the publishers.

Any person who commits any unauthorised act in relation to this publication may be liable to criminal prosecution and civil claims for damages.

A CIP catalogue record for this title is available from the British Library.

ISBN 9781398435896 (Paperback)
ISBN 9781398435902 (Hardback)
ISBN 9781398435926 (ePub e-book)

www.austinmacauley.com

First Published 2023
Austin Macauley Publishers Ltd®
1 Canada Square
Canary Wharf
London
E14 5AA

I dedicate this book to my friend, Wolfgang Weber, for his love and support. I also dedicate it to all the young people of the world. May they receive the proper foundation in their early years that will enable them to become good human beings with wisdom to build a better tomorrow.

First and foremost I would like to thank God for giving me life and allowing to write my third book, then I would like to thank my family in Kenya and around the world, after that I would like to thank my tribe the Maasai and the Sambaru for cultural heritage, then I would like to thank Kenya, my homeland, and Germany, my second home, specifically Berlin. In Berlin, I would like to thank my partner for offering me a luxurious home to write in and supporting me while I write, his support has been incredible. Lastly, I would like to thank Austin Macuely for believing in me and publishing my work.

Prologue

Rediscovering my sexuality and the joys of it after reconstruction was a blast, a force permeating throughout my body, through to all my veins and into the core of my being. It was something I only knew as a young girl growing up in the savannah of Maralal, a small village in north of Kenya surrounded by hills, where I use to after goats before I lost my sensation through a female a genital mutilation ceremony at the age of twelve.

After about forty years of living in a sexual desert, suddenly in me a force I could not control, a force stronger than anything I ever felt overpowered me that I thought I had to tie myself to the bed I slept in at night so as not to go out and sleep with everyone!

That which I had longed for, for more than thirty years was back, yet how in the world was I going to live it out when I was always made to believe that it is impure? To make it worse, a sudden desire of same sex experience! The mirror would break into a thousand pieces, and besides, it was against my faith!

Much as those feelings after reconstruction were awesome as I practically wanted to stick everything into my vagina, the result of the starvation of all those desert years, but the feelings were simply not pure!

How in God's name would I have been able to look into an innocent child's face, a child the epitome of innocence, the utter display of pure love? That would be stinking perversion!

Chapter One
After Reconstruction

Over 40 years later and I am in Berlin. A step I felt called to, a very difficult city for me, as my life has been plagued by a constant series of ups and downs, mostly downs, in a country where I feel alone surrounded by people that are determined to control me, people that do not wish me well.

Growing up in Maralal where I received primary school education from catholic missionaries from Italy, there, I got introduced to a western way of life, which resulted to a desire to go to the white man's country someday. Back at the time, it of course seemed like at the end of the world, a heaven which turned out to be a hell for me.

Now, It's over forty years later, and I am in the big wide world where I had longed to be as a child in the missionary school in Maralal, a village on the way to northern Kenya, an adventurous part of Kenya that is extremely interesting because the tribal people are disconnected to materialism and the evils of it that corrodes the human natural instinct.

Behind the library reading and looking at pictures of children playing with snow, it is a dream come true that I am actually living in the big wide world.

In Berlin where I live up to date, and sadly have no friends, on the contrary I feel like I have enemies and feel that everyone around me, even my dearest friends are against me scheming to destroy my life.

In Berlin, I feel as though my neighbours are always spying on me, believing I am someone they would never have an opportunity to become, perhaps as an African I have an innocence they have lost a form of originality. In any case after reconstruction, I only had one friend, the boyfriend at the time, a kind-hearted east German.

From pessimistic people from Germany, people that had been locked in communism for over forty years, a hard and cruel regime that had oppressed the human rights of the people living there, it was years after their freedom as the wall that separated the two Germanys were broken down, and still the people complained about everything always feeling short of something. My boyfriend, however, a good east German in the country I had immigrated to from Kenya to make my home is a different east German from the others who are real pessimists always seeing demons behind every bush.

The kind-hearted east German boyfriend supported me through acting school, which is what I had always desired from my childhood, to become an actress. He played a big role in my life, guiding me through the genital reconstructive process, a process that I had longed for, which I would not have been able to go through without him.

I was still in hospital when it became clear to me that as soon as I got back home, I would lose that which I had received! My sexuality! I did.

As soon as I left the hospital where I had undergone a reconstructive operation, my surrounding environment was very hostile, for little or no thought was given to emotional health in the capitalistic society I found myself in, a work orientated society that strived to earn a living with little or no concern for the spiritual and emotional life.

I was therefore regarded as abnormal when I started going to acting school, instead of learning a useful trade that would enable me to earn myself a living in my new country, another reason for discrimination which resulted to a gradual loss of my sexual healing I had received through the reconstructive surgery.

I felt like a criminal to be different, and thought it was an offence to be a sexy African woman, as if I would infect the east Germans with a virus just by them looking at me!

In the time after reconstruction, everywhere I went to I was booed, looked at angrily because I had just received a powerful sexual energy back after years of being in a sexual desert. I was filled with a dynamic sexual force, a magnet that made everyone stare at me. The reaction I received revealed to me the much-hidden pain of the repercussions of the second world traumas handed down by parents. The people loved to torment others, especially foreigners.

Immediately after reconstruction, I felt special, like a woman I had never had the opportunity to become, but already back at the hospital where I laid recovering after reconstruction, I feared I would lose that which I had received.

Kindly, the hospital offered me a chance to have a therapist, a very nice lady from the church which run the hospital where I got reconstructed, an offer I refused because I felt the therapist had no idea about female genital mutilation.

What does she know about poverty let alone female genital mutilation, the woman seemed to be too well polished for a wounded soul.

Instead, my intention had been to do research on my own in order to help myself and others like me. To begin with, my intention had been to go through a healing process, a process that seemed never to come, on the contrary, after reconstruction I found myself in real traumatic pains of rape, which triggered other pains from my childhood seeing my mother being beaten up by my father.

The first time, right after reconstruction, in a time I needed complete peace and the power of restoration to establish that which I had received, right winged people broken into my personal life causing me to become terrorised by fear, a feeling that was contrary to the peace I required for inner healing.

I was already dealing with the pressure of all the traumas

that had resurfaced in my personal life, as though overcoming all the traumas in my childhood was not hard enough, people started breaking into my personal life, that I felt unable to protect myself against their evil schemes.

If I had a mutilated woman as a therapist, it would have helped me to open up.

Indeed, shortly after reconstruction, I started seeing a therapist in Charité, a prestigious hospital in Berlin with a good reputation, the nice professor I perceived as a mother figure, helped me face some of my hidden traumas. There at the hospital, I encountered other mentally abused people from Germany who seemed to be more confused than me, although back at the time, I never asked what their problems were. There at the hospital, I experienced an unfolding of some sorts through painting courses that were offered as I continued to open up to the motherly figure therapist who actually helped me just by listening.

Once, I had got myself into trouble which was bad enough because I was already in probation after attacking a woman in the subway.

Suddenly, I attacked a man in the underground and broke his glasses!

A terrible commotion but the people were as calm as real Berliners. A bomb could be exploding next to them, and they would be cool, calm and collected. After the incident, everyone had to step off the train in the underground and amazingly I was suddenly very calm as though Jesus had appeared to me!

By the time the police arrived, it was hard to believe that I was the one that attacked!

Immediately after attacking, my realisation came back and I repented and prayed to God for help. Needless to say, I was sent to court where I was asked to take medication which I naturally refused.

Back then, I had signed a contract with a publisher and

was already in the last section of writing my first book, in no way was I going to ruin my creative process by taking drugs! I needed to face the process, the pain I was going through.

The result of refusing the court's decision was, I was asked to appear before a higher court of justice.

To begin with, I was living in a village in west Germany where I had gone to get away from the madness of big city life, draining away my very soul. In every corner advertising placard drawing my attention away from myself, the reason I moved to the village to be able to go back to my childhood to revisit the painful experience of mutilation.

In that time, I had shed a million tears, as well as laughed uncontrollably that the villagers must have thought I was mad, a stranger locked up in a room crying and laughing and never talking to anyone.

For the case, however, I had to travel to Berlin, the big city I had dreaded in the time while writing, in Berlin I had to stand in front of intimidating people who I felt had no sense of justice and imagined myself in prison finishing my first book!

This is the higher court of justice I finally thought when I got there! Good, I had forgotten the seriousness of it all!

I will pretend I have never been to school!

Like a little girl from the bush, in the midst Germans ready to tear me into shreds, oh and they wanted to throw me into prison? No way!

In my naïve business, I fought like a tiger!

The lawyer that had been appointed by the state to represent me just sat next to me taking notes of the process, I had to fight for myself, to make matters worse, there was an appointed interpreter that I did not need because I speak fluent German and because the interpreter felt not needed, she started expressing being uncomfortable by putting me down in the midst of the court process. Since it's not the first time I had been in court, I already had experience with incompetent government appointed lawyers, I therefore had to fight like a tiger for justice to defend myself.

Luckily, even though I missed the next day at court, in my wild naivety, I had totally forgotten that I had to appear in court the next day, to my surprise, I was acquitted of all charges!

There is justice in Germany after all!

The first time I got into trouble for lashing out at someone, I had spent a stressful day in acting school being bullied by classmates the whole day saying all sorts of things bad things about me putting me down German style to derail me from concentrating in acting school.

On the way back home to my east German neighbours not exactly the most peaceful place, it only took a few words to send my hand flying out of my chest and landing on a woman's face! Not only was the woman shocked, I, was terrified! To make it worse, blood was pouring down her face like I busted a waterpipe!

What of course I did not know was that I was holding my house keys. As soon as the police arrived, I shook so hard and was about to urinate!

By then, the woman of Arab origin, an intelligent strong and a confident woman was peacefully talking to me because she realised that I too was bewildered. I guess the woman felt guilty for provoking me. As two of them foreigners away from home bonded, you would think the woman would drop the charges!

Perhaps she wanted to teach me a lesson to learn to control my feelings.

After the attack of the men in the underground which was an attempt to teach Germans a lesson to be respectful, that is how i learnt from my mother growing up, I was beaten up when I was not respectful. In any case, it was the second attack and from the first attack and I was already in probation. As a result of the second attack, the authorities had to force me to take medication because they feared I would go on attacking people.

Around the time, many other unexplainable attacks were taking place, people going hammock, others driving into groups of people, I guess the authorities became perplexed it would bring them into trouble if they did not attempt to minimise the pain inside of me.

I did not take the medication, and still like a miracle, they dropped all the charges against me! My God did help me after all.

By then, my first book was coming out, a book about FGM, one of the biggest subjects in the world to this date, a book about atrocities against human rights, that many have to go through in Africa.

The authorities were probably afraid of sending me to prison, fearing I might become famous once my first book came out.

To be honest, it took a doctor from Charité, the hospital in Berlin where I received help to save my neck.

In spite of hesitations I felt, hesitation concerning the fact that they did not understand me, still I sought for counsel which was good for it was in seeing a councillor that saved me from being sent into prison.

From the hospital, I received an assessment that said, I did not only suffer from FGM, I actually went through so much. I did not only go through FGM and rapes, I also grew up with an abusive father who beat the hell out of our mother and that before our children's eyes.

Thankfully, as soon as my book came out, I was in a number of papers and received good critics.

This was wonderful because it did not only hinder me from going to prison, it also was a ticket for a permanent visa to stay in Germany, the country I love and always wanted to come and live in, the country that has given me a second chance after mutilation in Africa, the country where I discovered my hidden talents, Germany, specifically Berlin which has become my home.

As an asylum seeker with a criminal record, it would have been impossible.

Back then when I came to Germany in 2010, I was not the perfect foreigner economically, one who is already a princess when I came to Germany. Then I would not have needed to come here. I came because I was escaping oppression, poverty and hopelessness only to end up in a bigger oppression of the Neo-Nazis, oppression of a spiritual poverty worse poverty than that which we have back in Kenya or in Africa. For spiritual poverty can be hidden what many do here in the western first world countries, whereas material poverty cannot be hidden.

It became an incredible great torture for me going through the spiritual poverty and I believe I speak for many immigrants who flee from war oppression and hunger only to end up in a worse form of oppression especially from the less educated in the society that have no appreciation for other cultures, the right radicals of the western countries.

The subject of discrimination in the public places became a daily confrontation, and this was worse because I had depended on welfare which made me feel as though I deserved the discrimination. Exactly that inferiority feeling gave my hosts the rights to treat me the way they wanted to in public places, they loved my inferior thinking and really worked on putting me down.

I discovered pretty early what very famous people go through with the tabloid always at their back, always being watched! Big brother is watching you, you better be perfect or we will tell on you!

Like them, I also wanted to hide and did not want to be confronted with the rapes, or maybe the repercussion of it and other traumas.

Yes, I want to live to experience sexuality, not with others, with myself and with my husband in the future, a man that would love me as I am and beyond my worst fears, or in spite of my worst fears.

Sometimes I actually thought I would never marry. The possibility, my worst fears, that through rapes I might have been infected with a terrible disease scared me to death and I felt that it might blocked my future and ruin my chances. Then again the trust that God knows of my fears, and that in spite of them, would give me a husband, a man on my side to protect me from the abuse of men that are interested in destroying me as a woman, especially against the Neo-Nazis who drove me to the point of insanity keeps me standing.

I will live to overcome FGM and teach others to overcome it themselves.

I will to live to make our world into a better place, God knows we need it.

Given the doubt of a possible end of my life as I went through a lot of fear, it was the fear of death that actually gave me that extra zeal to want to live beyond my fears.

Wanting to live gave me the zeal to fight against the pessimism of Neo-Nazis and others that did not mean me well and I choose not to allow myself to be controlled by their dark thinking threatening to take my sexual healing, the chance to rediscover a new life.

I want to live for myself and victims of FGM and other forms traumas and discover my fullest potential and teach the victims of FGM the same.

I will stop FGM and help others to overcome the repercussion of it.

For this, I have to go through the path of healing in whichever way I need, sexually, emotional physically and spiritually a difficult path in light of the pessimism of mentalities in dark negative thinking that surrounded me all the times which makes it difficult to unfold, as a matter of fact, it radically affects my development but I am a strong woman a fighter and I am a winner.

Chapter Two
Seeking For Acceptance In Germany

Being insecure, and the people insecure, I sought for acceptance from others which they could not give because they did not know themselves neither did, they love themselves. I wanted to pick up fragments of my life piece by piece, question after question, word for word.

Instead, I felt like garbage as people threw their ugliness on me and I became totally broken, covered by fear and shame. I also became angry because I expected others to do their homework of cleansing their own shame which they redirect on me through discriminative demeaning gestures!

It's of course easier to dump rubbish on others. To point dirty fingers on others instead of looking into one's own hidden mess.

Back then, I practically had no idea of how to defend myself and all those people who did not love themselves attacked me causing me to hate myself.

They saw me as a threat, someone coming to take their jobs, in the worst case, someone that had come to ruin their lives. How were they going to love me, saying good you are here? They themselves never learned to love because their parents were too busy making money. This is sadly a problem for every immigrant leaving their country to find refuge in the foreign world.

Are they being too hard? Am I being too hard?

How in the world am I ever going to find inner healing surrounded by such a hostile environment of people hiding behind masks pretending to be very intelligent but in fact they are stupidly running away from themselves, their hidden traumas in order to protect themselves from the pain inside of them?

The country I have come to live in, is proving to be almost impossible to feel at home because I do not understand the people I have come to live with, people that always protect themselves from being real, from being that which they were created to be, loving. They have lost the ability to be sensitive to the needs of others, instead it's a greed-oriented society with almost everyone putting themselves first.

From Africa, I had always perceived white people to be better!

Ugliness! Hypocrisy!

On the one hand, initially, the cold calculated superiority made me feel intimidated and therefore inferior now however, I do not feel inferior anymore, but back then, I was terrified of the mental games of putting each other down. Yet back then, even in fear, I just did not find it right to be at the receiving end of hate, actually I do not believe anyone should be at the receiving end of hate, instead of hate, back then, I longed for the innocence of pure love, a state of being in which I could unfold sexually in all purity.

We in Africa are much better I thought, not realising I was falling into the same trap of pride.

At least in my Maasai upbringing, we had much emphasis on love and oneness. I received a lot of love from my aunts growing up, which became important in the new country, it also became the nightmare because the people I always thought were better, were falling so much short of my expectations.

There is no unity here, no purity, just a rat race to make the most out of time regardless of who one might hurt. A rat race of looking good outwardly but inwardly not knowing who one is.

In any case, that which I was seeking, that which I had in the tribe from my aunts growing up before female genital mutilation, that oneness, the magic state of being growing up in nature is missing. Here, the communities are practically empty because everyone goes to work to make a living. In some societies, no one is left at home whatsoever, so that there is no one when guests or children come from school, practically no one, a desert in regards to spirituality that makes one fearful and through the fear one becomes a victim.

It eventually became clear that only the natural tribes and artists possess that which I am looking for.

Back then however, in the new country I came to make home, I of course did not know what was hidden behind the masks. I did not know, they were individuals crying out for the same, like that which I was and I am still crying out for myself.

Pure love, respect and acceptance!

Eventually I came to find out that the country I have come to live in is dominated by hidden cases of incest, child sexual abuse, and hidden atrocities that people dare not talk about!

My fellow human beings here like me are hurt by past pains only they were taught to oppress their feelings, unlike my African blatant openness, which is actually a stumbling block. It's because of my openness that I perhaps fall prey to attacks.

Its good not to dwell in the past, and I have come to understand that the past requires to be brought into light so that it cannot stand, one must turn the pain into power instead of running from it or oppressing it.

I will not go into the blame game, what good is that?

Besides, isn't it my arrogance that brought out the worst in my neighbour, my pride, thinking I am better?

Part of the fear the people have generally, is the fear of the unknown, the fear of death.

This was heightened by the influx of the many refugees that streamed into the country in 2015 and later through the corona epidemic, the Ukraine war, the oppression of women in Afghanistan and in Iran to name but just a few of the struggles we have faced as a human race in the last times.

Back then 2015, I felt sorry for the people here, having all the peoples of the world coming to their country to depend on them. On the other hand, I thought we bring our cultures with us, our originality which enhances and brings diversity in the cultural scenes in the countries we immigrate to. Back then in 2015, it sometimes became clear for me to understand the bitterness of the right radicals, and as long as I took money from the government, I also felt guilty of depleting and not giving.

Back then, I was living on my own, without family and friends normally in a big city, which naturally leads to being conceited and arrogant.

My intention in coming to Europe had been to take to back what the colonialists had taken from us as well as to give back what the western first countries had lost. A human heart. They took our culture and raw materials they took our identity, our African heritage and caused us to ape their ways, and in doing so, they lost their humanity. My intention in coming here had been to bring the wealth back to Africa to build us of communities that had been destroyed by colonialism, and eradicate poverty caused by global warming. My intention had been to restore our stolen heritage so that Africans can live in dignity once more rather than going against each other dying alone in poverty and miseries or through injustices of corrupted politicians.

In all of that I looked for answers outside of myself, which of course became hard to convince my pessimistic east Germans that I lived with at the time after reconstruction of change, who am I an African to suggest change, especially when I became the strange neighbour that went to acting school.

You are so different, my neighbour, a man living above me once said.

I must have called the police more than two hundred times on him as I felt he consistently stalked me. Actually, because of my traumas, I had psychosis and I did not know it. Generally, in the state I had been in back then, my attempt of healing Berlin was a desperate cry that I needed the inner healing myself.

In fact, the emotional healing of the city, which I did on a daily basis had been out of fear and desperation because I felt traumatised by the emotional pain hidden in Berliners.

Later on however, after I had started to experience inner healing myself, the healing of the city started to stem out naturally and through that, I could give back, indeed I attempted to give back what the German people had lost, Joy and a form of a spiritual awareness as Germans are more in their minds and less in their hearts.

After reconstruction, I had just transformed to a butterfly and felt as though the world was against my new colours, against the unfolding of my soul the newness being, the woman I did not know. My soul longed to fly into greater heights, to achieve the impossible and make the world into a better place, but I felt as if everyone around punished me. They punished me for daring to rise beyond the norm, for daring to dream the impossible, which provoked envy and jealousy in others not knowing they have the same chances to transform their pains, they could achieve the same spiritual state as I achieved or even better because they are at home here.

That certainly provoked discomfort in my situation in my neighbourhood in the middle of Berlin living with the east Germans.

The ugly looking street not far from Friedrich Strasse one of the main streets in the former east Germany, a street that reflects the hearts of the people that live here where back then, they perceived me as a bad person just because I had big dreams that have been since shot down to almost nothing.

Why are you so special, someone else angrily asked me in a supermarket underneath the block of flats where I lived, as if I stopped them from thinking big.

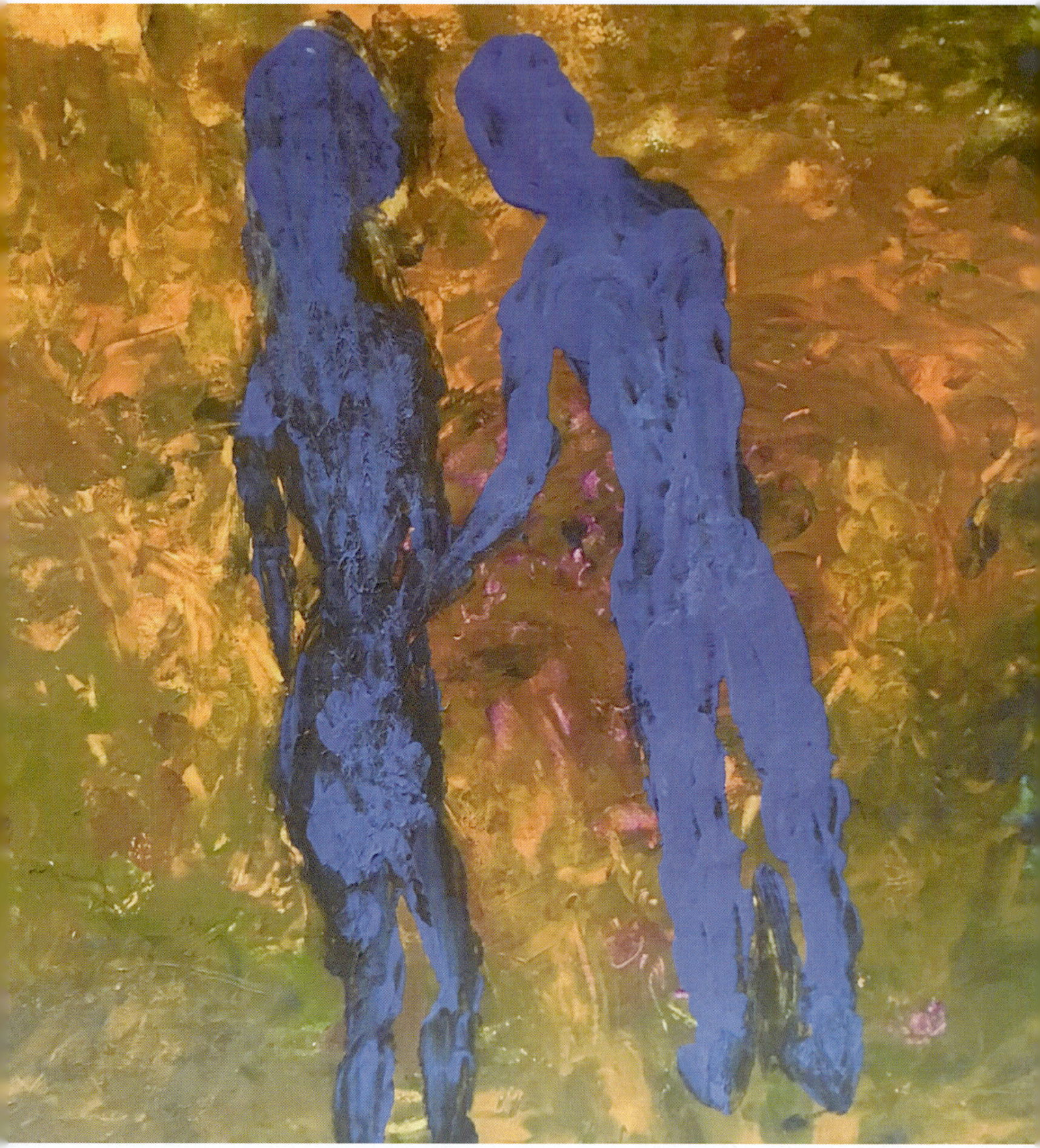

Chapter Three
Further Inner Turmoils In Berlin

Back then, after reconstruction, I was of course also not sensitive to other people's needs, I only thought of myself and felt better than everyone around me which made others feel bad. I can understand why they felt angry and attacked me verbally.

I had not yet discovered to be humble is to be broken, in the end the east Germans broke me, and I came to learn to appreciate them for that. Back then, I was of course too hurt to realise that.

I had been hurt by mutilation and rape before I had come to Germany in 2010. And since I did not receive enough love in early formative years growing up, I only thought about myself, which is normal when you are traumatised. Everyone around me were also thinking of themselves and fighting for themselves. I was like everyone around me, I was right and everybody else was wrong, and had a big ego with everyone else's ego of course bigger, everyone fighting to win stupid arguments.

After my first book Fluegel fuer den schmetterling der Tag mein Leben neue Began came out, Wings for the Butterfly the day My Life newly Begun, my journey through FGM, I thought my life would drastically change and I would become famous and important and have a great impact. I Therefore moved out of east Germany leaving the energy of struggles a reflection of hidden pains. I did not know my expectation were going to be short lived, I did not know I would end up in a worse situation that I was in. At least in east Berlin, I had an affordable flat!

Maybe I should have been happy that the right radicals did not burn my place down in east Germany, as it was the case in many refugee homes at the time.

I sometimes actually felt I needed to leave my door open, which is how I grew up in our homestead in Maralal back in 1974. I grew up amongst the Samburu, a tribe related to the Maasai, that separated with the Maasai and remained in northern Kenya where they mixed with the tribes in northern Kenya.

In the manyatta, our homestead where we lived, my aunties little huts had no doors, one could always walk in and sit in the peaceful hut sensing a beautiful presence when all the grownups, mainly aunts were out fetching fire wood or water, the children looking after goats on those rare occasions when the manyatta was completely empty with only the presence of being.

I would simply walk into one of my aunt's huts, sit there, sensing complete presence and peace with myself. It was equally good when the aunts and my cousins were around in the daytime and when we were not in school or looking after the goats in nature. Then, we would play with the dried-up cow dung in the middle of the manyatta while my aunties would make jewellery and talk about their good old days when they were girls before they were mutilated, the good old days when they had fun with their warriors.

Of course, I reacted that people came into my flat, I called them idiots and worse, the reason I attacked people! A natural reaction especially also because I had been raped.

Some of the people naturally could not understand my pain, they simply thought I was a bad person, just as I could not understand their pain! Why they felt they had the rights to cross my boundaries by breaking into my flat, I totally did not understand.

With a better environment, I felt better inside.

In the new environment in west Berlin, the negative emotions soon calmed down and the voices in my head stopped. This gave me space to receive sexual healing that I had learned to oppress in the midst of the surrounding pressure that seemed to have gotten out of control.

In Kudamm, one of the most glamorous and expensive street in Berlin, with all its big names, I felt good, people seemed to have other problems. Back then, they were sad about the present situation in the world, that children in Africa are starving and all the other world problems and helpless they could not really do anything to help. In general, however, a much more relaxed environment.

In the new environment, people seemed to celebrate me as an exotic person, and I even started to work on my second book, an African fairy tale about a princess that sought to end Female Genital Mutilation in her tribe. Then, I began to perceive myself as someone that stands for humanity, someone that brings about healing and restoration, especially in connection with FGM.

In Kudamm, on the western part of Berlin, I became surrounded by labels, beautifully old ladies with their lovely dogs taking a stroll on an autumn afternoon as it was autumn when I got there, relaxed and happy people that lived in the present not rushing to get anywhere or always being busy like I have experienced Germans to be.

In Kudamm, I felt captivated by a friendly kind of capitalism which of course boosted my ego making me feel important.

I still had nothing materially, in fact, it did not take long until my landlord discovered that I had no money. Because my rent was expensive, I was depending on the free food given to poor people. After my landlord discovered I had no money, he threw me out, and without an affordable flat to go back to, I was really homeless!

Back in the flat in Kudamm, there was a mirror in a corridor where I would sit with my legs open and massaged my whole body ending up with massaging between my legs until I would get a number of orgasms; it was my clinic to recover sexually where sexuality with myself become normal like breathing.

It was back in East Germany that just touching myself felt

dirty. I felt I was living in the midst of people that had been sexually abused in their childhood and was picking up the wrong vibes in the air, vibes that made me feel ashamed and dirty.

In Kudamm, the feeling, the sexual desires were pure, the most normal thing. I felt one with myself and with the universe and started to learn to reconnect with the power within.

However, a bridge between my mentor and I evolved which resulted to less and less support from him, leading to problems with the landlord which led to being kicked out.

It was sad, for the flat had become an oasis where I was recovering from the repercussions of female genital mutilation and other forms of trauma.

I knew the flat was expensive, but I felt it was worth the amount I was paying, that is 1400.00 Euros a month, that I sacrificed for the sake of restoration.

A small compensation for all the lost years, years after female genital mutilation and rapes and growing up with an abusive father. I was desperately trying to find home in the midst of the madness I had come to, the traumatised city of Berlin where many are traumatised and do not know it.

Suddenly, I was out in the street without money and a place to go to but with a book and much peace.

Having written a book was good, at least I knew I was helping someone with my story!

After I was kicked out, I first moved to a hotel and then to an older lady I met who was kind enough to offer me help. After losing my mother at an early age of twenty years, I appreciated the woman's gesture. Little did I know there were hidden motives. As soon as I discovered it, I left immediately.

Upon leaving her flat, I met another lady who also offered me accommodation on the spot like the first lady. She too had issues with sexual abuse growing up, issues that I did not want to meddle with.

All my life, sexual purity had been important to me, and as a Christian even more, and in the city of Berlin where anything is allowed, it became even more important, innocence is what kept me, and it became more important at the same time gave me a lot of strength.

Was it our pains, our traumas that bound us together?

Was there any normal person in the world anymore?

In that time, after I was kicked out of Kudamm, it seemed all my friends were people with some kind of sexual abuse in the past! Why was I attracting the wrong people in my life?

One thing became clear, even as we in Africa have issues with female genital mutilation and other atrocities, I became aware of the hidden issues here, sexual abuse in the formative years.

On the surface, things looked good but, in the core, the repercussion of hidden trauma starts to show with people showing the ugliness without any specific reason. The ugliness is evident in the way it corrodes their lives, it causes physical and emotion pain, a real call for spirituality to intervene, a cry in a country where less than ten percent of the population go to church nor seek some kind of spiritual guidance.

Having been deceived as a child to think that female genital mutilation brings purity, I'm very well aware how important formative years is and very protective about children.

Wrong foundations bring about dysfunctional humans, who in turn bear dysfunction children, the circle must be broken. Children have the right to receive pure love! It seemed everyone I was meeting had issues of past sexual abuse and was acting strange in one way or another.

Like bombs waiting to explode if not dealt with, these hidden traumas represented by many that do not wish to face it can explode, sadly these cases are represented in our societies many of which are hidden.

Luckily, there is spiritual help we can reach out to which got

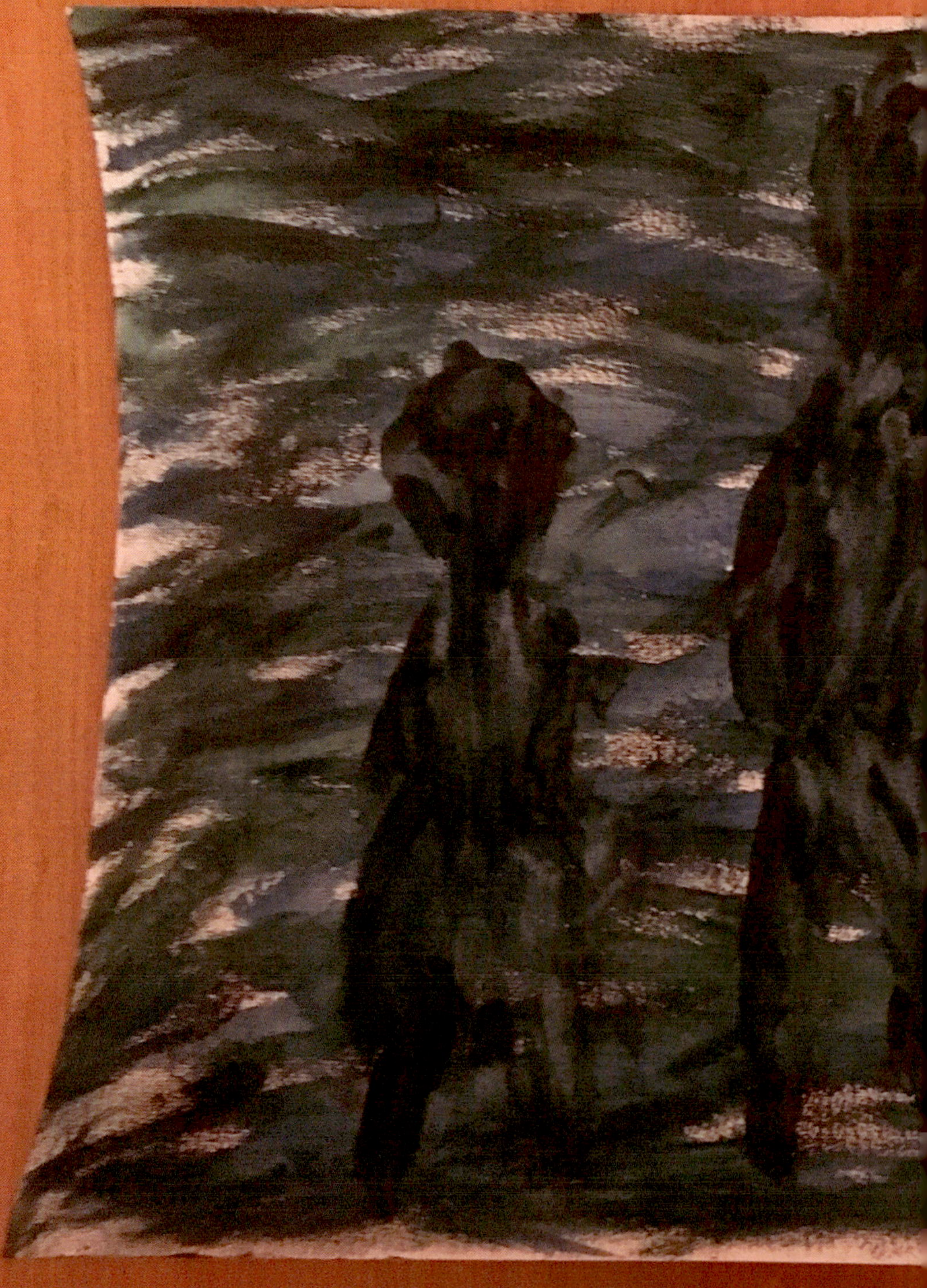

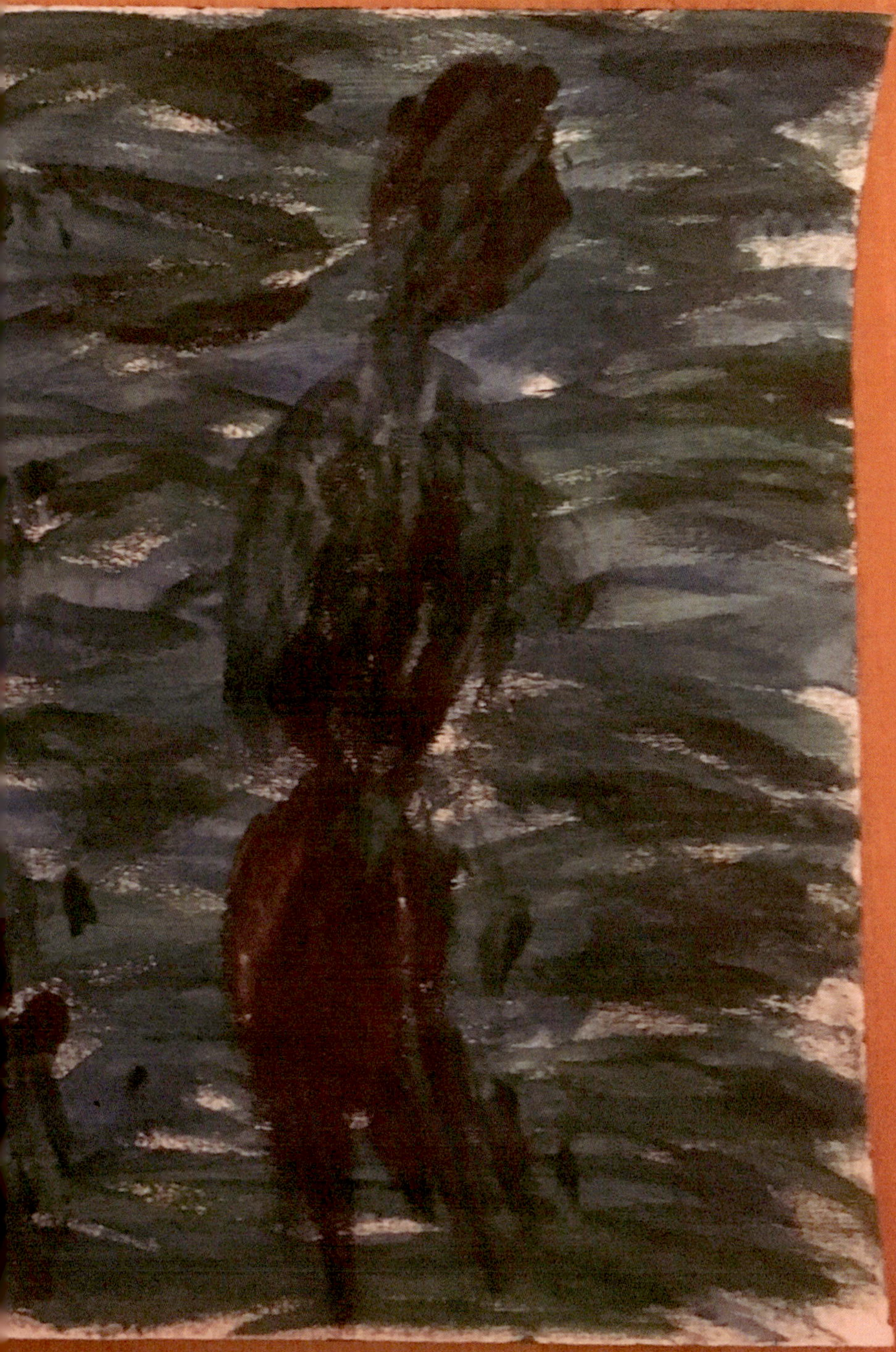

the better of me, I do not know what I would have done without it.

I believe that much must be done to heal the past, and in this country of Germany more consideration must be directed on healing the past. The fathers came from the second world war and were clearly traumatised and passed it on. However, they did not receive help to heal their past and until now many old people in Germany don't even dares speak about their past, it's a taboo.

One way or another, these undealt issues of their hidden past must have been passed on to the children, and the children's children and they too don't dare speak about it.

Instead, we who are traumatised become experts with outward defence mechanisms, which makes it easier to point fingers on less fortunate people displaying weaknesses.

Chapter Four
Repercussions of Traumatisation

I remember a time, when I was still very hurt. As a repercussion of trauma that I wanted to take a machine gun and gun down people in Alexanderplatz, a square in Berlin central.

Instead, I tried to become a people knower, a people whisperer, whispering to bring healing to the people in Berlin, a voluntary job I gave myself. Sometimes I felt like the mayor of Berlin going around healing people in the subway, a city with a traumatic past having gone through two major world wars, and with the wounds of the second world war still evident in her walls.

In the next place I ended up in after I was kicked out from the expensive flat, I rented in Kudamm the main street in Berlin, the woman and I eight years older, actually become friends until I felt she betrayed my trust and I left again.

She had opened up to me about her father that she had indirectly killed, a father who had been the most handsome man, an example of one that had obviously inherited traumas of the second world war in Germany, and passed it to his daughter by abusing her sexually since she was three years old!

She completely forgot her childhood or erased it from her mind, and to be honest I was very shocked that she actually killed him!

Perhaps it was to relieve him of pain because he was in an old people's home and had dementia. She did not want to see him deteriorating for the loss of his memory. Frankly, I think there was hidden rage in the act, pain of the lost innocence through him. Together with a doctor they gave him medication. She did not want to go into specifications, and I did not ask.

After he passed away, she became the little girl that had been deprived of mother's love. Naturally, the mother was not happy of what she did, coming between her and her husband.

Eventually, after leaving the woman's place which I did after she touched my breast for the second time and I had the feeling of killing her, I ended up in a refugee home, a place I had always wanted to avoid.

In the natural, my pain became extremely intensified living in a surrounding full of control and manipulation from the people with trauma of wars trying to reinforce that into each other's because they did not know how to be free.

Our pain collectively clashed, and it became a worse hell than that of the east German and of hidden haters. It was difficult to figure out who was worse off! I even sought refuge from Nazis in a pub where they met a real desperate attempt for restoration between cultures, the couple running the pub were a mixed couple of German and Turkish origin.

I remember often staring at trees, to feel their presence in order to evade the darkness of my own thoughts practically surrounding me.

Nature became my comfort which is what the authorities had in mind by bringing the refugees there I guess, an area idyllic with nature everywhere, lakes, trees, birds, and a lot of fresh air. Even though it is in east Germany with a pessimistic type of people living there, a right-wing-oriented people, they left you in peace if you are not troublesome and accept their mummering.

The one thing I still could not do there was to get personal with myself and unfold in my newfound sexuality, as the men in the refugee home were hanging on my every move like hungry hawks.

Equally as I could not unfold at the friend's flat who had been abused by her father, and in east Germany where I lived after I was reconstructed, I also could not unfold at the woman's house who I trusted as a mother figure and in the Refugee home.

In the refugee home, people knew that I had gone through reconstruction, and though I attempted to find my freedom of expression as a woman with an unfolding sexuality; the Islamic culture was in contradiction to the freedom I was attempting to attain.

There, I felt the pressure to be myself and stand to my new freedom to being sexy on one hand, on the other the hand I felt the pressure of being stalked by the Muslim men. I eventually become very upset with my mentor, the man that had helped me write the first book for letting me end there and felt he had purposely done that to oppress me and my sexuality.

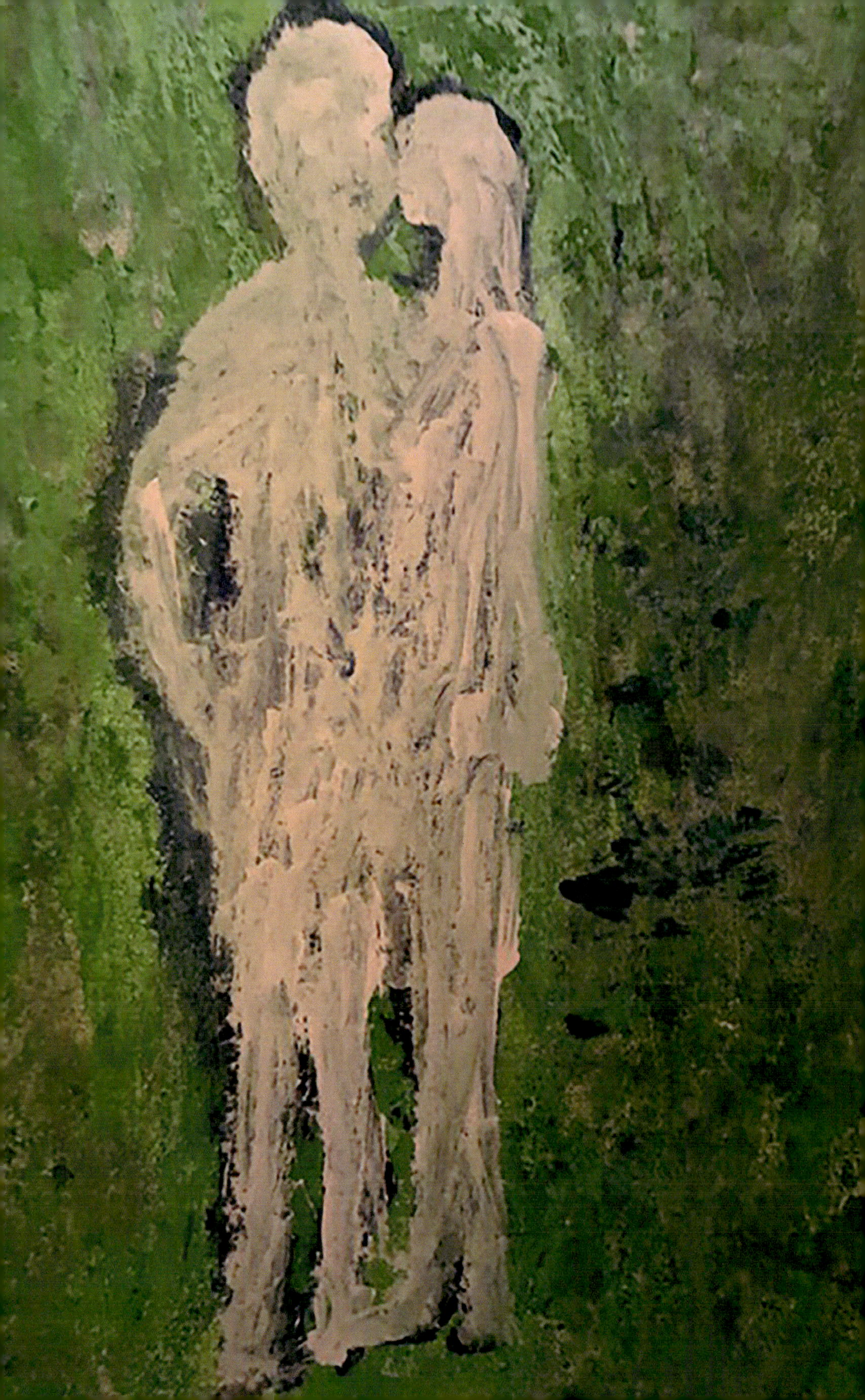

Chapter Five
The Big Wide World

The heaven out there I thought where I want to be, this was my first attempt of becoming a global citizen after my first visit when I was a teenager before going back to Africa to seek for my identity after I found religion in London at the age of twenty-one. Little did I know what that meant.

Back then when I left Kenya for the first time in autumn 1983 to come to England with an Englishman we met in Nairobi on his posting by the British army, the Kenya I knew was dominated by white people that seemed to be better. Generally, I found the mixture of black and white people living in Kenya to be a beautiful one. Back then, it was evident that the white people were doing well, they drove better cars, lived in the best part of town and always had enough to eat.

I was living in Nairobi when I met my ex-husband who invited me to go and visit him in England; a chance I jumped at thinking I was going to heaven.

The heaven where my hell broke loose.

Where I discovered the nightmare of sex, where I started to fake orgasm so as not be useless as a woman, where we eventually got married, where gladly the marriage came to an end because I never felt he was the right man the man I wanted to spend the rest of my life with.

We were in Germany when our marriage ended and I moved to England where I met Efua Dorkenoo, an activist against FGM who taught me that FGM was wrong so that I began on my journey of dealing with the subject confronting my own situation as a victim of mutilation, a process that led me to seeking for spirituality as I felt useless as a woman.

I ended up becoming a Christian in a church in London after

doing a faith course and found my meaning in being a child of God.

After eight years, I realised that heaven was not in Europe, and went back to Kenya to convert my family members into Christianity. There, I spend almost twenty years before I came back to Europe. My family were shocked when I came back, shocked that I had actually given up heaven in Europe, they were more shocked when I got rid of my British residency, a document which others would sell their souls for.

After giving up my British residency, even though I was doomed to poverty for the rest of my life back to Kenya after living in London, in Kenya, I lost my status and in the eyes of my family and people who knew me, I was a loser. I still did not have proper education, for I never received a secondary school education in the first place, still I felt I was doing the right thing in God's eyes and trusted He would make sense of my life in time. In fact, I had heard a still small voice that told me I did not need education back when I attempted to study social work in London, before I went back to Kenya where everyone was struggling to get their identity and self-worth based on education and away from their natural identities as Africans.

In Kenya, I had only been there for several months, and I had already given up my British residency that people thought I was mad, I was therefore forced to live with my sister Esther also a victim of a worse form of FGM than I had gone through.

I tried to help her come to terms with her inner struggles but because I had not yet dealt with my own struggles, I was unable to help her. Actually, I had no idea about the destruction in my own life caused by FGM.

The only thing I knew was FGM is wrong, and it needed to be stopped, which I preached like a mad woman everywhere I went. In my then religious frenzy, surely many thought I was caught up in a new sect, that preached against FGM. In Kenya, I desperately clutched to my religion the only thing I had and bible and preached to people around with a team of missionaries where I found myself discovering poverty in the forgotten northern Kenya and other problems we were faced with yet we were not in the position to help and asking God where He is.

Back then, I had enough time to pray, so I prayed a lot for Europe, I remember praying especially for the children in Europe and feeling sorry that their parents did not have enough time for them, I of course had no idea concerning the history of child sexual abuse cases in the western world, that too many children lose their innocence too early in their lives, many of them not daring to open up for fear of being judged.

I remember I use to feel the same when I first discovered that FGM was wrong, I was a teenager, and it would be the last thing I would confess!

No, I did the opposite.

I pretended, and made myself look outwardly good, focusing all my energies in outward appearance. I even faked orgasms in my marriage which I walked out of later, to live with a rich man, where I bought myself expensive things to hide the deep sense of meaninglessness I felt within.

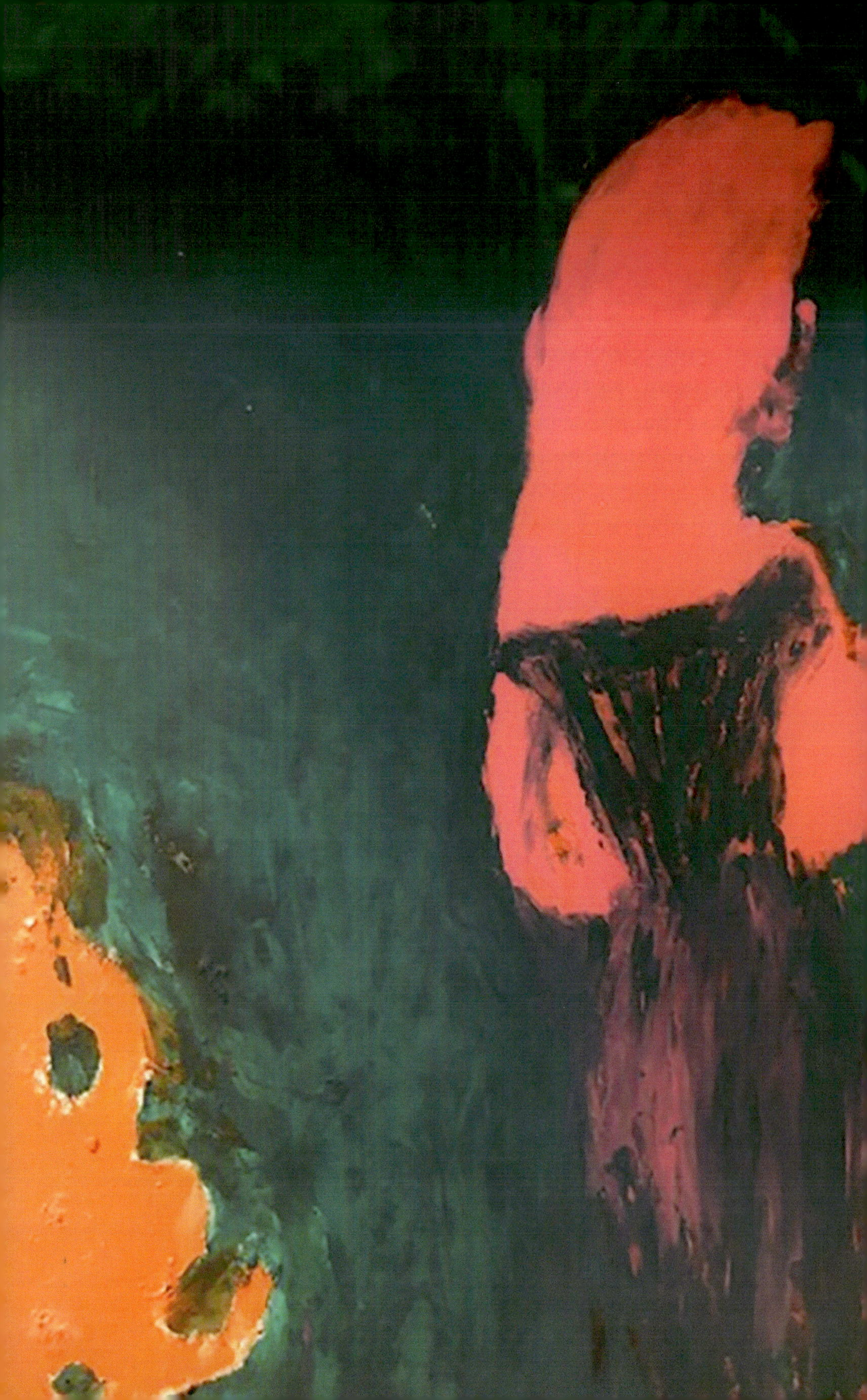

Chapter Six
Mutilation

This chapter is about mutilation, and I hope to assist those who have gone through it and are standing against to know what they are doing is good. In this point I believe to have information that might help because I have gone through it myself, anyone who goes through FGM and is aware that it is wrong has information to help the others still in the dark. My intention is to guide others with my own experience.

Frankly, I often wonder how much potential must be hidden in them that have undergone female genital mutilation or other forms of trauma, potential they are not aware of or will never be aware of. To be aware of the potential as a victim of FGM you require to get to the root of your own trauma in order to acquire the wisdom that could be attained out of the experience.

Sadly, instead of reaching to the root of the problem many victims of female genital mutilation and other traumas are passing on the pain to their children, I say this with knowledge of the many that do not get to the roots, many of them in Africa that still practice female genital mutilation.

The Three Types of Mutilation

SUNNA

The type I went through that removes the outer skin of the female genital leaving half of it is called sunna. Although it's bad as my life was brutally damaged as a result of going through it, it's not the most severe type of FGM.

My sister Hellen and I went through it in a clinic in ongata rongai which is not very far from Nairobi on that dreadful day when our mother walked us there to initiate us into womanhood. As we walked back home after the ceremony, I do not even know how we managed having just gone through what affected thirty years of my life, the robing of the better part of me.

This type of mutilation is supposed to leave you with some form of sensation, they believe, however it left me numb.

After our mutilation ceremony, my sister was married to her husband Lemaiyan, the only man she has ever known physically, and said she felt him until later in life when she suddenly stopped feeling.

In my case, the sensation started coming back in my life at the age of thirty-seven when I started desiring to feel after a long time of feeling nothing totally nothing. I started to touch myself again many years after mutilation where I hated my private genital, the touching created a longing to get restored.

That my sister Helen and I narrowly escaped the traditional ceremony of clitorectomy, the second type, is a blessing in disguise.

I do not want to make it sound like it was okey to go through sunna, it is not and my sister Hellen and I went through a lot of rage, for Hellen who is two years older, her rage was immediate after the ceremony. My rage was silent, I became withdrawn, depressed, I felt alone, and when I ended up in a marriage in England, it was a nightmare because I had to fake orgasms night after night, I felt nothing but pretended to be very sexy.

CLITORECTOMY

My sister Esther and most of the girls in my school where I grew up in Maralal on the way to northern part of Kenya went through clitorectomy. Most of the tribes' people in northern Kenya apart from the Turkana mutilate their women putting them through clitorectomy. This involves removing the whole of the genital of the woman, the clitoris and the skin around it. In the traditional ceremony, it is mostly done in a celebrative manner; the highlight of my childhood, back when we did not know it was bad on the contrary. The warriors and the girls would be assembled to sing, dance and later have sex, while one of them would be losing it and being married off afterwards.

The traditional girls that undergo the operation, would then be led to her husband's home the next day having to walk for God knows how long.

In Kenya and in Africa, millions of women have gone through this mutilation, most of the older generation, indeed worldwide it is believed that up to two hundred million women have gone through female genital mutilation, and I would say half of those went through the second type which is clitorectomy.

INFIBULATION

The third type of the mutilation is known as infibulation. This happens mainly amongst the Somalis and at a very early and tender age mostly at the age of five and which is very cruel. Who in the right mind would put their children through such cruelty. It involves the cutting off of the clitoris, the skin around it, and stitching thereafter.

Eventually, the girl would go through another trauma, having to be cut open on her wedding day.

The purpose of stitching is to ensure virginity on the day of marriage, a cruelty that robes the children of their childhood and future as woman to enjoy their husbands, many of these women become very aggressive as I have observed growing up, I never knew why until I grew up myself and in a foreign country suffering the repercussions of the trauma and talking to many immigrants that have gone through the same.

I have mentioned before that I have cried a million tears for myself and others, and I cannot imagine what women like

Waris Dirie and others go through, women that experienced infibulation, tyranny of the worst type and still live to tell.

It is time to put an end to this barbaric pracice now!

It's time to fight for our sexuality, fight agaisnt men that want to dominate and dictate us, men that beat us with us with words, beat us physically and emotionally, demean our worth, it is time to fight against cultures that dictate against our bodies, fight against evil desires to manipulate and control us!!! Stand up and fight now!!!

We are able to if we stand and fight, and only this way there will be restoration!

I believe, even to the worst type of female genital mutilation can be restored with a strong will to overcome no matter what. Like a tree which brunches are cut, and which grow back, our bodies are able to recreate through breathing exercises yoga and learning to forgive and let go of the past, ultimately there is hope for everyone, when they turn to their deepest part in the soul, the broken subconscious to release the pain they went through.

What happened should not dictate our lives, instead it should propel us to be better people, overcomers instead of victims, women that focus within to awaken the power in them, rather than focusing on the damage of the trauma.

This is ultimately what not just the victims of female genital mutilation should do, but victims of all forms of traumas.

I say this with personal experience which I still go through to this date, and with experience of others like my sisters which I have personally observed or refugees that I have met in Europe especially in Berlin who come here and face the glorification of sex to a point it makes one feel worthless a feeling I know too well.

Life is not just about sex, it's about pure LOVE. A human is not worthy because they are good or bad in bed, otherwise children will not have meaning in the society, but in fact the best part about the society is the young generation because of their innocence. Investing in them is the main focus in life, not because we benefit from them, the only way we benefit from them is through their purity which strengthens us.

In the countries that have not yet started discussing about FGM at all, it is important that people start discussing about it on tv, in schools on radio especially in schools because most tribal people respect education.

The hidden princesses in Africa must rise and take a stand against mutilation in these countries, for there is no victory without a struggle. They have to do that for their future and that of their children.

Grownups have done a lot of mistakes and attempting to restore on behalf of the future generation will not only bring healing into our own lives, it will also encourage us to view ourselves in a better light and help us gain better self-esteem. Is our duty to encourage the younger generation to stand up for themselves, and say no to atrocities like FGM, and other forms of oppression, lies that seek to oppress us as humans, making us lesser than we are supposed to be.

We have many problems in Africa, poverty, sicknesses and many others to name only few, we should not add ourselves more problems like female genital mutilation.

It is my hope that in the countries that still practice female genital mutilation, homes, for girls that want to escape will be build, for they will need them. It is the right of a princess to know their own body, the home of their soul, their possession given to them by the Creator to live a holy life. In my trips in Kenya where I speak against mutilation, I encourage the princesses to live holy lives and touch themselves when they have sexual desires but wait for prince charming a good man that is deserving of their purity.

This teaching is required as part of sexual education especially Africa, where we have other problems like HIV Aids.

Purity is therefore required and to wait for prince charming the man worthy of the girl's purity, is a good teaching that will go well with the community's desire for holiness.

In my trips to encourage the girls, I tell them, saying no to mutilation or other forms of oppression, does not rob them of worth as a princess, on the contrary it enhances their femininity.

I personally have gone through much of rejection in my life and I rise to encourage as one that has gone through much rejection.

Projects that fight against mutilation must teach the girls to remain confident in the midst of the persecution they will receive because of standing against a lifelong tradition. In these countries, consideration and offers of compensative supports to the girl's parents must be given to minimise the out casting of the princesses, the young daughters of Africa the pride of our future.

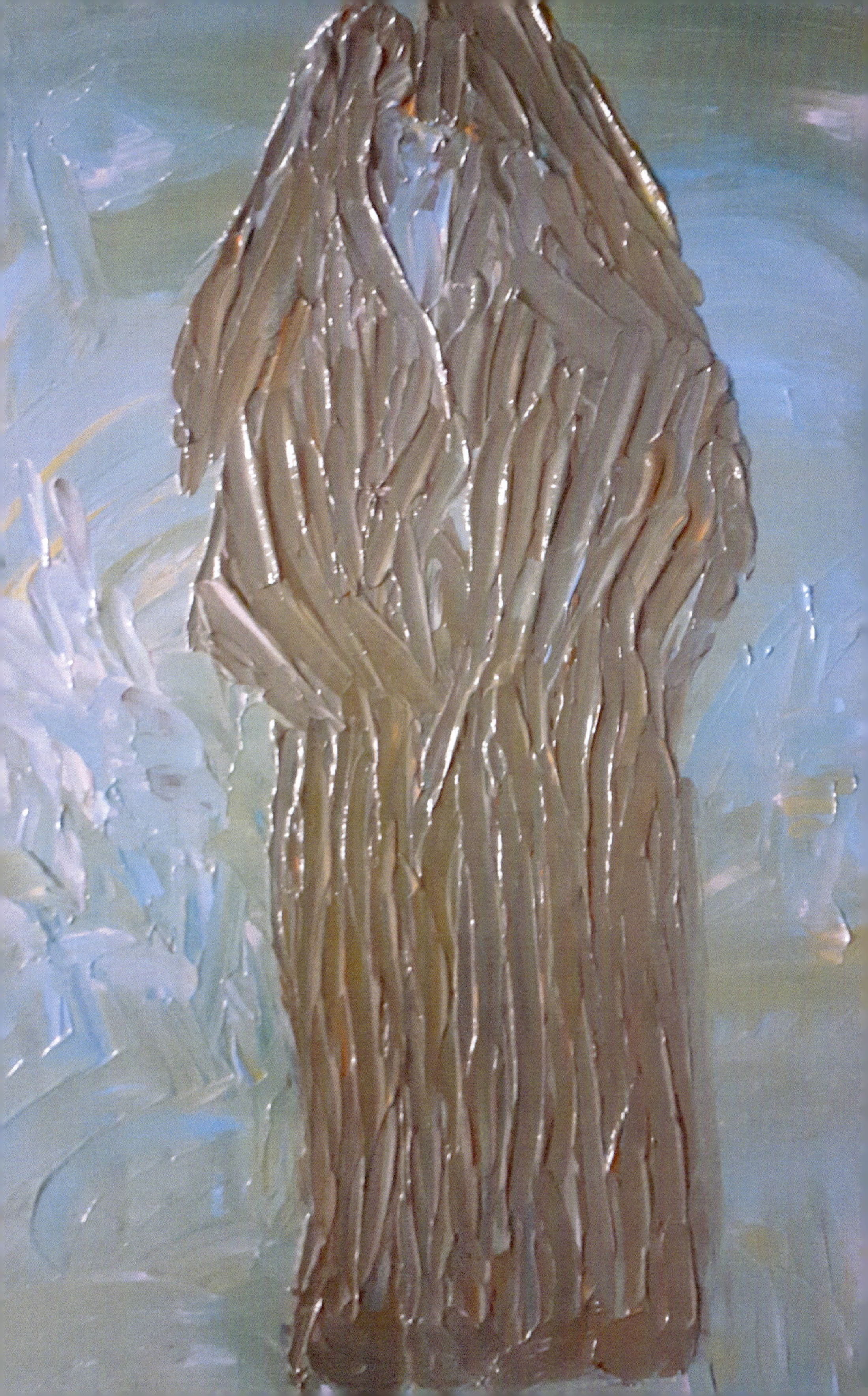

Chapter Seven
The Lion and The Ostrich

Growing up our father loved to tell us stories whenever he would come to visit us in Maralal.

We loved his stories and grew up listening to them. He did not just tell stories, he also took us to the bush, into the forest near our home and sometimes when we visited him where he was stationed with his troop seeking for bandit hiding in caves, he would take us for walks in the bushes there.

This story is one of his stories about a lion who stole his neighbour's children after shitting on his own children!

Once upon a time there was a lion and an ostrich that were neighbours and live harmoniously next to each other.

One day, the ostrich who had planned to go hunting to bring her children food, asked the lion to look after her children.

"Yes of course the lion said, trust me, nothing bad will happen to them." As soon as the Ostrich was gone, the lion became sick. Back then, there was an epidemic in the forest and many animals were sick. At night, while sleeping, the lion who was also sick with diarrhoea, shit on his children covering them with shit.

"I do not like my children anymore, they are not good," he said.

"I will go over to ostriches' children, they are pure and clean, and I will swap them and exchange them for mine!"

The ostrich went on hunting, totally unaware of what the trusted lion was up to. "The lion will eat your children," some monkeys said to the ostrich.

"Noooo, he gave me his word, the ostrich said, and I trust his word, he is the lion, the king of the jungle."

Three days later, the ostrich came back, to find the lion's

children instead of her own, to make it worse the cubs did not only stink, they looked pitiful and dejected.

"Oh, you poor little cubs," the ostrich said. "Did your father leave you here?"

"Where are my children?"

"We do not know," the lion's cubs said.

"Our father brought us here and said you are our mother now!"

The ostrich was infuriated, flapped his wings and rushed to the lion's den to have a word with the lion.

"You conniving fooI, I trusted you. I should have listened to the monkeys in the forest that warned me against you!"

"Where are my children? I want them back immediately without delay!"

"Ha, you are nothing but a bird, and lucky to be alive. The hyenas should have eaten you out there in this dry season. Your children are those stinky creatures. My children are these innocent and clean small little creatures that use to belong to you."

A quarrel between them started that lead to other animals in the forest discovering about it.

It was not long until all the animals got to find out about the heated discussion between the lion and the ostrich and called for their shaman, the prophet of the animals to mediate.

"Let's have a meeting to discuss this like reasonable beings," the shaman and the prophet of the animal said.

"In three days, we will all gather here, and come up with a solution to this problem."

The three days were over in no time, in the meantime, the ostrich took care of the lion's children as though they were her own.

Before the three days were over, the lion and the shaman had met up.

"I will bring you meat for the whole dry season if you let me win," the lion said.

"Well, of course, you need not worry," the stupid shaman said cheaply.

"You are the greatest," my friend.

The Gathering

"We are gathered here to find out if these are the lion's children," the shaman said.

All the animals were attentive, fixed on his words as the shaman was speaking.

"Whose children are these?" he asked, pointing at the ostrich's children next to the lion.

"Of course, they belong to the lion," they all said, fearing the lion. Besides the shaman might prolong the dry season and their children would die of hunger in the ongoing drought if they said the truth.

"The birds belong to the lion," even the elephant said!

Although everyone knew that the lion had stolen ostriches' children, out of fear, they all said the children belong to the lion, until a squirrel was asked.

"I have a request," the squirrel said.

"I would very much like to give my answer but I'm small and require to be placed on top of a termite hill so that all the animals can see me."

That is what happened. All the animals moved to a location which enabled them to find to a termite hill where the squirrel was placed as the animals waited anxiously to hear her.

Instead giving an answer however, the squirrel started by asking questions.

"Since when, did the leather bore feathers?"

"Never," the animals said.

"And since when did feathers bore leather?"

"Never."

"It is therefore clear, that the children belong to the ostrich!"

Suddenly, the lion jumped to devour the squirrel, but she was faster; she had already escaped and hid. Quickly, the animals called for the elephant. "Use your trunk to get the squirrel out of the termite hill, we must punish her for telling the truth," the lion said.

"Why punish the squirrel for telling the truth?"

"We are all too afraid to face it, but the squirrel even though she is the smallest, said the truth and must not be punished, on the contrary, she must be rewarded for being the bravest of all. We have allowed ourselves to be manipulated because the lion is powerful, but the squirrel even though she is the weakest has stood up against the giant and won!"

With that, the ostrich received her children and the lion was advised to take his children to the river and wash them. The squirrel was free, and no animal was to endanger her in any way ever again.

DIFFICULT TIMES AND THE NEED FOR FORGIVENESS

In my time in Germany, I have experienced my worst discriminations, ugliness in its truest colour from lion like character that thrive on messing up people's lives. Seeing the right radicals in his true colour, and I see how much the history of this country has messed up the people, a history that desperately requires healing and restoration.

Every culture has dysfunctions they have to overcome. I do not want to go into our the dysfunction we in Africa have gone through, I have covered some of it in the earlier chapters.

Having said that and in connection with the lion that messed his children, this is a good point to bring in forgiveness towards the ones that have messed us, the lions that have used their power to destroy our lives when we were children, at the work place, or in a marriage. All of us need to forgive in life as all have issues in connection with our dysfunctional cultures and our upbringing.

In connection with my own life, I had to learn to forgive, and I did it by speaking it out towards my father and mother. I think I had to forgive my father a hundred or rather a thousand times before it became a reality, before I could actually set my him free and feel love and appreciation towards him instead of rage. I remember the first time I felt the urge to forgive him. The result is, I suddenly stopped smoking.

The next time I knew I had to forgive was when I met Efua Dorkenoo, an activist against female genital mutilation and through her started to discover that female genital mutilation what I went through was wrong.

After that, I was overwhelmed with rage and again it took forever to forgive my mother, a rage that boiled down to other spheres of my life, affecting my relationship to others.

A never-ending process that when you are traumatised you have to keep doing, you also have to forgive yourself for reacting to the pain inside of you and letting it ruin your relationships. I for one have issues with trusting and because of lack of trust I found that I have always ended in abusive relationships, or I personally become controlling or even physically abusive as a reaction to the pain inside of me.

Likewise, I found out that many are the issues this country and like in many other countries as every nation have their own issues, wounds from the past are evident, the darkness that requires the healing light of forgiveness and letting go of the past in order that it will not overshadow our futures.

I believe the atrocities that happened in the second war still have their emotional affect here in Germany and the country's wounds can only be repaired by looking, really looking into the people's hearts and souls.

This is a requirement in every nation especially also for us in Africa, in the countries that still suffer from female genital mutilation.

I was very ashamed of the fact that my female genital was

mutilated, and I am still ashamed when people say I am a liar when I speak about sexual healing, and I am not healed. It's a traumatising personal journey that I or other mutilated women that go through a reconstructive surgery experience we do not have to prove to anyone that we are healed.

Personally, I believe we have to be open about what we are ashamed of which is already a big step of courage that needs to be recognised, it will encourage us to move to the next step which is forgiveness. In connection with the victims of female genital mutilation and other traumas, THIS IS A MUST.

You have to forgive your culture, parents, relatives and everyone in connection with your trauma.

There is no other way.

Broken people and I used to belong to the category must FORGIVE, in order to emerge a winner and I am writing with the intentions to help You, help US achieve that.

Do not let yourself remain a prisoner forever, rise up and take back your life!

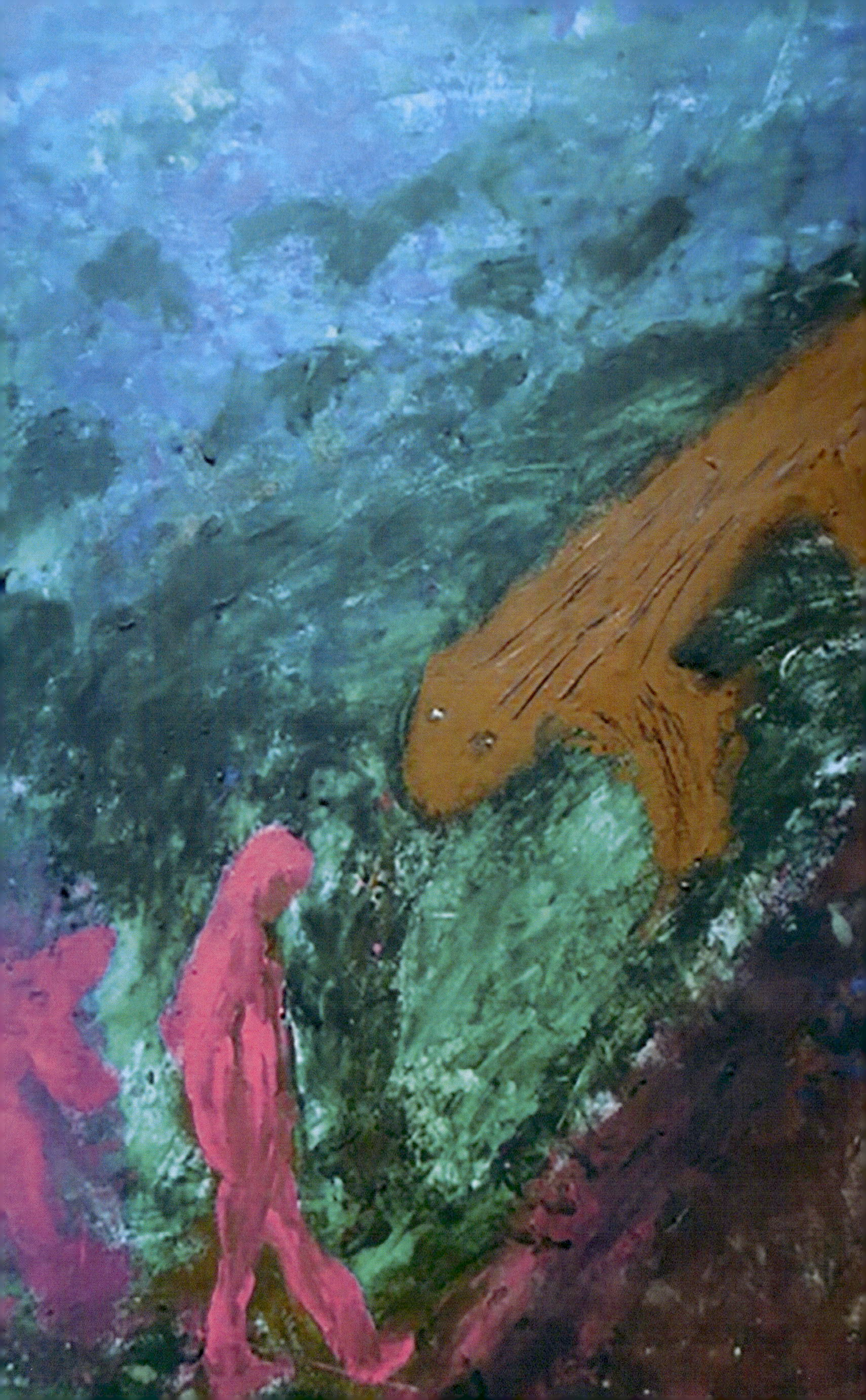

Chapter Eight
The Wild Maasai

Who would ever think that the little girl that walked for ten kilometres a day to fetch for water would ever raise to write three books to make a better world. It's a miracle that I am grateful for and if it's possible with me it's possible with anyone else. Anyone, especially the people who go through experiences, injustices against humanity, can raise above it and use their bad experience to change the world. People in Ukraine, women in Afghanistan and in Iran can rise up to become the heroes of our world. Back then after my family became poor due to the separation of my father and mother, I would have never imagined that I would make anything of out of my life let alone write books. All I saw back then was darkness that became the door to light in my future through which I could write and inform others of the dangers of female genital mutilation!

Growing up amongst the Samburu tribe in Maralal with my sisters Esther and Hellen and our cousins of the Samburu tribe enjoying the beautiful nature back when Maralal was still small and less populated gave me the natural back up to do the good things I did in the future. Going through what you are going through, being oppressed, mistreated being bombarded by bombs in Ukraine living under the Taliban regime in Afghanistan might be the door of your story to write about and enlighten the world.

How many countless of conflicts did I have leading to a difficult life, especially back then after the mutilation and walking for miles just to fetch water.

Here, forty years later into the future there is water, but my soul is often empty a poverty worse than the one I had back then when I walked for miles to fetch for water. A spiritual emptiness where I sometimes wish I could have a pool of spiritual refreshment to dive in to escape the hypocrisy and lies draining the life out of my very soul.

What is the point of luxury when one's souls is starving, a luxury that some people here have or think they have, while in fact people are starving a starvation caused by the egoism of the western capitalistic world in a world in which there enough food to feed every human being alive yet many are starving to death and living in utter poverty.

Forty years later and my soul is still longing to find home. Yet my home is when I write to inform others of the injustices of the world. My home is when I uncover traditions that harmful to us as a human race. My home is creating and provoking discussions to do with taboo themes. My home is when I protect the children of our world, the future generation. My home is when I am one with my spirit and one with the eternal Spirit of God then I am home anywhere in the world.

It was emptiness the emptiness which came through FGM that drove me to England where I got married when I first left Kenya after I was mutilated, and equally, it is emptiness that led me out of the marriage.

It was emptiness that drove me to seek for the meaning of life in the modelling world in Berlin after my marriage, and it was emptiness that led me to study social work with the hope of reaching to help others to find meaning through that.

It was emptiness that led me to become a Christian after realising that life had no meaning, and it was emptiness that led me to give up everything and go to live in Africa with nothing in order to find meaning in nothing.

Now the question is, have I found the purpose and the meaning of life?

I would have to answer the question with going back to the past.

I believe the purpose and the meaning of life is connection

with every part of one's life and going through it step by step. Its sequence after sequence, moments after moments accepting the moments good or bad and turning them into power that leads to the meaning and the purpose of life.

The purpose of life is not in sexuality, otherwise we would all become perverts, the purpose of life is in connection with our true self, which is our spirit, it is in connection with everyone and ultimately it is in connection with God the creator of everything.

Our lives are like wells, the deeper we dig and turn our bad pasts into gold, the more meaning we find in life and the happier we become. Failure to do that, we become depressed and depress everyone around us. We are filled with wrong emotions of envy and are guided by evil intent.

Bad experiences do not have to turn us into bad people.

We are to look for people we can open up to, teachers that guide us to dig deeper into ourselves, spiritual leaders, people through whom we could attain the ultimate point of inner spiritual awareness to find answers to all our questions about life. My faith as a Christian is my path that answers all my questions an important path without which I would not have made it this far.

Concerning our body.

I believe, men would like to perceive us women as sexual objects. I believe they would like to reduce our worth to nothing in order to feel good about themselves. Maybe I just have not men the good men yet.

It seems, most of the men I know grew up with fathers that mistreated them or mothers that sexually abused them. These men repeat the cycle by taking their frustrations out of their women. For the sake of their children, women should rise above their men's dysfunction by understanding their men's history. It's hard, especially in Africa and other third world countries where women depend on their men, nevertheless I think they should not react with aggression, but with getting a deeper understanding of what the problem really is. A spiritual woman that is not depended on her emotions will take charge of the spiritual guidance of her family when the man is weak and lead him out of the dark. Naturally, if they are able to women should walk out of abusive relationships to build themselves and their children a safer refuge, thankfully in the western world this kind of help is available.

The Maasai

The Maasais are nilo hermites and originally came down from the Nile into northern Kenya over about three hundred years ago. There is no written history concerning the Maasai only fairy tales about their origin. One of their believes is that all the cows in the world belong to them the reason the warriors use to attack other tribes and take their cattle for themselves.

The tribe is divided in a hierarchy with the elders of the tribe in charge of politics that defines the tribal life. The council of elders consists of older and younger elders, followed by the Elmuran the warriors and then the boys about to get initiated into warriorhood who would move with the warriors taking the cattle to find pastures, the women and children are in least in the hierarchy.

Because the women are not highly regarded in the tribe, the reason why FGM is preferred, in order to oppress their position, at least I believe that was the initial aim, most men, if they can afford are allowed to marry as many wives as they wish, the reason why they often opt to looking for younger women.

In the tribe respect is very important, the reason women cannot question what happens to them. This is thankfully not the case in this day and time. Now, the Maasai women in Kenya are rising up, a real shift of consciousness especially amongst the Maasai and the closely related sub clan of the Samburu my father's clan. I would like to believe that the collective awareness amongst my father's sub clan the Samburu is partly inspired by the rise against FGM internationally in the great wide world and especially also through my biography. In any case amongst others like Josephine Kulea, Nice Nailantei in the Maasai and the Samburu tribe non-governmental organisations like AMREF with their activists have done tremendous great work leading to a collective shift in the consciousness of the tribal women's lives, that I never thought would possible this soon.

After the shift of consciousness around the country of Kenya, the tribal women are opting to rite of passage for their girls' initiation instead of mutilation, which is done collectively and which is a constructive step indeed a joyful ceremony to perceive a change for the better in the tribal culture.

The rite of passage done collective is a culturally acceptable ritual an important step leaving the girl intact without robing her of her youth and heritage as a woman with she would grow to become as well as giving her the cultural identity.

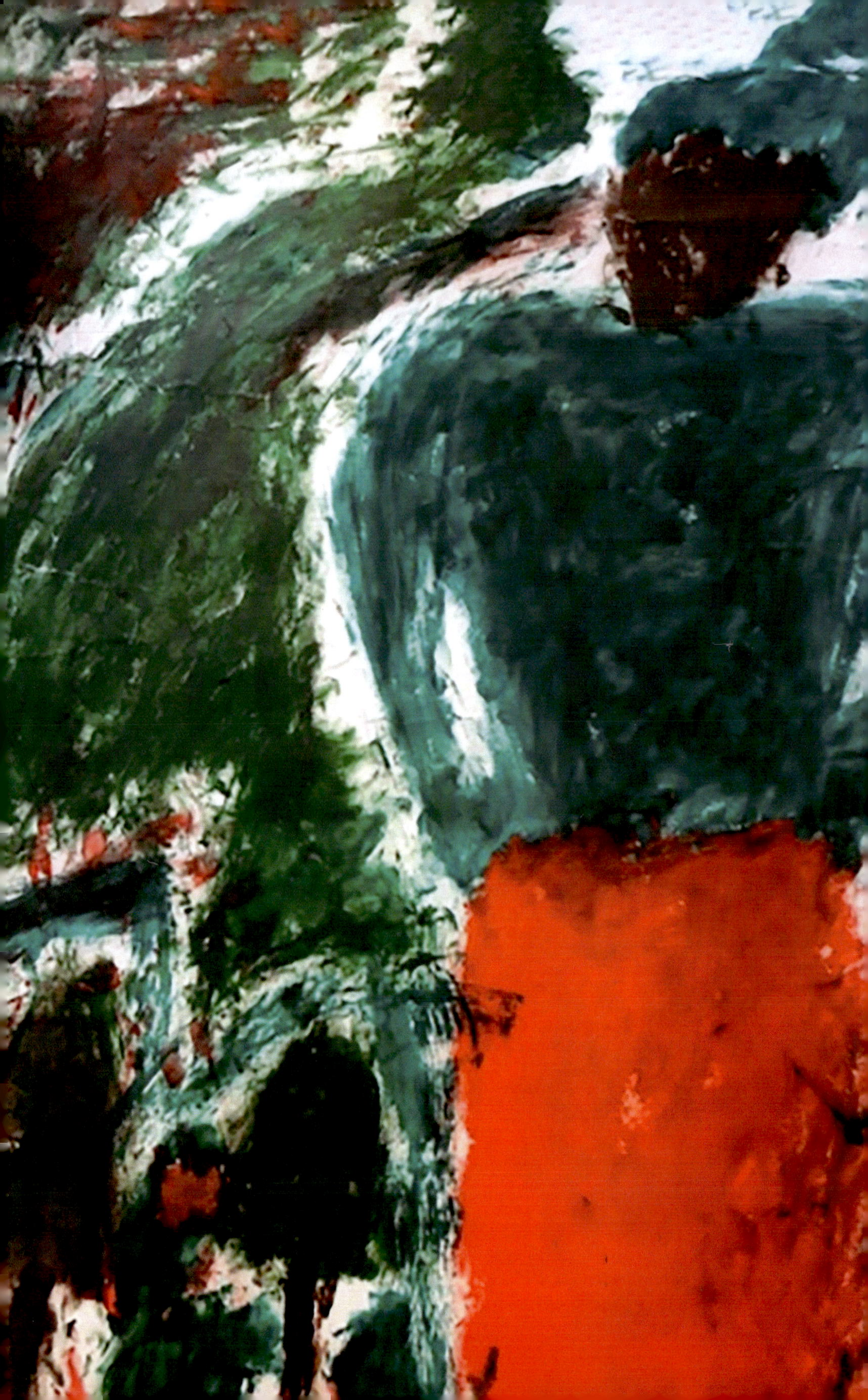

Chapter Nine
Light in A Broken World

I attempt to use my life to expose our strengths and weaknesses, with the hope to help us look within ourselves, not that I have attained perfection far from that, but I beat up my ego falling and waking up to the good and bad in life that makes us the people we are when we are able to live a humble life admitting when we are wrong.

Through our ancestors many are living in a fallen state of being and have been in the same fallen state for generations.

We are living in a world that is full of darkness portrayed in our selfish ambitions of corruption, with corrupted people wanting to grab and are never satisfied.

How can one laugh about FGM, child abuse and other atrocities like hiltler with all the people he murdered! How can one laugh at Putin for the invasion of Ukraine, how can one laugh at the women suffering under the oppression of a regime that does not allow them the freedom of expression?

What do I mean by laughter? Is it to laugh at mean people deliberately trying to harm or sabotage the innocence of people because they do not possess means to protect themselves? In Germany, I sometimes had to learn to become mean because the egoistic generation beat up my innocence and tormented me all the more because of being a good person.

Because of being good, I have been considered as stupid and badly taken advantage of!

In fact, they even stole money from me to name but a few examples, stalked me, spied on my mail on my phone, because they think I am naïve and blind, they have even said false things about me! I did not laugh about it at the time, I still do not laugh about it.

Yet sometimes, I laugh at the inability to show greatness, but I am also not great because I sometimes cannot love them and turn the other cheek as Jesus said!

Instead, I laugh at their weaknesses, and I refuse to allow myself to become hateful! Yes, I realise this kind of lifestyle is egoistic and the only thing to do is laugh, a good advice to everyone undergoing suffering of some form through dominating or manipulating powers in some way. Laugh, it is good therapy. I totally admire the people of Ukraine, and I have cried with them. I do not know if this applies to Ukraine, but the best advice is to forgive and love our enemies but to keep a distance from them because they delight in hurting others.

I feel sorry for their blindness not seeing their wrongs and unwilling to admit to themselves that they wrong especially in the cultures that practice forms of control that dominate, like Russia.

The characteristics of the bad lion like characters are destruction through manipulations, intrigues, control, oppression all these and others should not frighten or intimidate in any way. When I first came to Germany, this forms of treatment from people would drain me of all strength and sadly I became a real victim. Now I just laugh and refuse to be derailed from my focus to do good and create a better world.

It is sad that controlling goes on a normal basis, in schools, in workplace and at home with families and wrong friends. It made me question myself about whatever happened to the real purpose of us as humans to love and serve each other. How much controlling must go on until we are broken down by a higher power to bring us back to ourselves?

At the point I'm writing this, the world is going through an economical shut down through the corona virus and the invasion of Putin in Ukraine, for me as an African and for many Africans or Syrian people that have already been through many crises, it's another crisis and perhaps because of it we are able to accept the shutdown easier but we still fall under the category of being the ones that will suffer from it the most. It's a time when the truth seems to belong to the powerful and not to everyone, a time when the truth is not the truth, but a better argument is the truth, a time when the truth is punished and lies celebrated.

A time when FGM and other important issues that affects us as a human race are pushed to the side as culture to be accepted. A time when our voices as activists are getting weaker. Patience is required in these times in the dark season where only hope appears to be the light at the end of the tunnel.

Concerning sexuality as a mutilated and a reconstructed woman, yes these subjects are still important and should not be forgotten themes.

I tell myself, never to write another book about sexuality and I would like to advise anyone that has gone through a reconstructive process or is thinking about it not to do the same, not in details, especially reconstructed people should remain a private matter. In my case it was not, and exactly that on top of other stresses are the reasons that blocked my unfolding.

Being open about sexuality has caused some in the society to force and turn me into an object of their pervasive fantasy, that I would not allow myself to unfold. It's a bit like a small girl discovering her sexuality and grownups entering in to mess the process. In my case, because I'm already grown up, the inner mechanism shut down as soon as I sensed danger.

It's sad that sex does not have the sacred meaning anymore it ought to have of godliness, something divine.

I feel sorry for all those that have to go through reconstruction, only to go through the hell I went through, with everyone wanting a part of you, like you went through the reconstruction for them. My intention is to emerge a winner and give talks in the future to encourage especially victims of FGM and other traumas. Hopefully in the future clinics will be built to help women who have undergone a reconstructive process to establish themselves in order to maintain the new passion and not lose it under stress of high expectations.

Turning pain into power.

The human race is great and created with great potentials that is hidden inside of us.

This is the reason I can sometimes understand when others are envious of each other. They see you and feel the lacking in themselves because they are not connected to their own greatness. They need to get in touch with their deepest selves in order to do their own discovery.

I call it the treasures of the darkness, ouch, turning pain into power.

Some of my friends have actually blamed me for lying about reconstruction saying I lied about recovering when I did not. I do not know what people were expecting. A bombastic sexual bomb that made them get an orgasm just by looking at me!

The society must show a maturity of being able to allow reconstructed women to peacefully find themselves without listening out to them, is she having sex or not, did they really find sex now?

After reconstruction, I often thought of sex symbols like Marilyn Monroe, and I did not want to be turned into her pushed to exploit myself by people searching for heroes to admire. Another reason why I oppressed the healing process and like a snail I crawled back into the shell in which I lived in for years where I felt save.

I know however that there is a tiger inside of me, and in the right time she will emerge.

This is not just my experience; I have met a few women that have gone through a reconstructive process and they shared the same experience.

They are lost or oppressed through the process after reconstruction, in many cases it's not lost its only hidden for loss of guidance. I cannot imagine what pressure they might go through in their hostile societies, what rapes when there is not sufficient guidance.

Sadly, there are no clinic where women can go to after a reconstructive surgery to spent time healing, with guidance of teachings of meditations and breathing techniques of connecting with themselves. You come back into a society that oppresses women's sexuality or perceives us as sexually objects.

I do not want to think of what the Somali community would do when their women go through a reconstructive process. It really has to be a collective work of restoration that require shifters of consciousness that do some overcoming transformative work of understanding the spiritual place of a woman divinely not culturally.

After my first book came out, there was much I could have said to the politicians concerning establishing more for women that go through a reconstructive surgery. Practically every reconstructed woman I met had their sexuality and lost it afterwards. I think that is waste of money, and more trauma for the women!

Unfortunately, my book did not receive the reception we had hoped for. The resonance we had hoped for that would have created a revival to enable me to fight for the victims of FGM to and establish clinics, fitness centres where Victims of FGM can do yoga and learn how to feel themselves and maintain their sexual healing before going back to normal lives after a reconstructive surgery. The women must learn to be at peace with themselves and allow their sexual unfolding, they must learn that is okey to feel sexual.

Healing after a reconstructive surgery must become a pure collective step accepted especially in the communities that are against women's sexuality. It must become normal and the men must be taught how to love their women back to healing. In the same way as the paradigm shift in Kenya concerning eradication of FGM has been a collective matter, everyone standing up together and saying no to FGM collectively and I am glad that I have played a role in the shift in a small way, sexual healing or restoration of women's sexuality must be accepted and treasured in such communities that oppress women's femininity sexually.

Sadly, up to this point in time, there are still many countries in Africa and in the World that have not even dared to start questioning FGM, let alone start on the journey of healing process.

It is going to take major campaigns of raising of awareness, from us all as and we require our sisters worldwide to give us solidarity by standing with us. Yet ultimately it is us who have gone through the trauma that will have to stand and eradicate our problem ourselves.

I know that from my own experience.

We are the ones that are going to bring about a collective shift by making noise and saying no to child abuse, no to rapes, no to oppression no to manipulations no to domination that demean our growth as worthy humans, we must turn our darkness to light!

In the midst of difficulties such as we are going through on earth at the present moment, it is a calling to our gentle and loving selves, which will give us a chance to turn our destiny around for better and not for worse.

I very much admire people like Nelson Mandela who regardless of all the turmoil they went through they were still able to emerge and make an impact in the whole world!

It's time for those great heroes hidden inside of us to wake up.

It's time for people to turn their pain to power.

We have no need to be hypocritical hiding behind hating on each other.

In transforming our pain into power, we can begin to turn darkness into light and gain power for us as a human race.

It's a war against the darkness of this age. A war against the mean generation fighting the innocent generation.

Are you a mean or an innocent person?

A love revolution is what we require, a pure love revolution. For the prince of darkness, love is not pure, and through him many have suffered under the impure love.

The prince of light is the author of love, pure and non-egoistic love, love that sacrifices to allow others to shine. Love that speaks no evil against their neighbour, love that is not self-seeking.

The prince of darkness and the prince of light.

Back in story of the lion and the ostrich, we get to learn about the lion that messed his children.

A perfect example is that of female genital mutilation in Africa. The parents do not mean to harm their children by putting them through the practice, they believe it's a good thing, the same applies to many here, messing on others because they have been messed on, parents ruining their children because they were ruined by their parents.

What we go through brings out a generation of dominated that dominate, manipulated that manipulate, controlled that control, mistreated that mistreat, unloved that hate, and oppressed that oppress others making our world into an emotionally dysfunctional world full of pride and arrogance.

Unfortunately, many have been the children of this dark thinking they inherited from the bad lions of the world that have their evil permeating through our populations with child abusers, and mutilators running around everywhere as though it is normal. Sadly also, the oppression goes on in unexpected places where one does not expect it to be.

This kind of thinking is also found in churches where priest abused children in boarding schools, and those unknowingly going around abusing others spreading perversion and wrong foundations to a point that makes it almost normal to be abusive. It is a tragedy which requires healing. The perpetrators of abuse must realise their need for healing so as to break the circle in their lives.

It's a particularly vulnerable situation for children that miss their parental pure love as they easily fall prey to perpetrators, the lion like characters that mess on others.

To mention good examples of ostriches like figures in the story, examples of father-like and mother-like figures that protect their innocent children. Amongst a few of them, people the whole world admires, Nelson Mandela, Mahatma Gandhi and many other hidden heroes men and women that work hard to look after children and help establish a good foundation in their lives. The teachers in kindergarten and in schools the good parents the good relatives to and all those who are kind to children to them we owe many thanks that no words can express.

In my quest for truth, I came to realise that true leadership is giving power to the people and not taking it, and because I have been through a lot of pain in my life, it has become my desire to give power in the form of writing.

And only hope my influence will grow, in which case I begin with telling You African Princess that the most important aspect of your life is Your innocence, Protect IT!

Grown up are not always good.

They do not love you when they ask you to do what is not right, when they touch you in a wrong way. You deserve pure love! Say no, and know that the law is on your side, there is no need to fear, say no to female genitle mutilation! Say no to child sexual abuse.

THOUGHTS FOR DAILY ENCOURAGEMENT

It's better to be Noble than to be small minded. Noble people are firm confident and loving.

Noble people are respectful, their worth is not derived in making others small. Noble people are connected with their true self, the well of wisdom inside them.

Noble people know themselves, they have no fear of the uncertainty, of the unknown. Noble people inspire, they motivate. Noble people overlook wrongs, making the best out of mistakes. They are humble, forgiving and just.

Noble people possess insight, understanding and wisdom. They equip, encourage and support. Where there is doubt, they restore hope, where is fear they restore faith, where there is war, they restore peace, where there is hate they restore love. The noble are rare gemstones to be held in high esteem.

Noble people are leaders by example, they guide, empower and draw people out of problems, out of themselves, to be themselves. They are wise, taking advantage of given situations to create change, change that enhances the cause of humankind.

Noble people are rooted, finding their depth in an awesome eternal God, small people find their depth in destruction, which they widely spread. Noble people spread an aroma of pleasantness that enriches everyone in their surroundings.

The Nobles are humble, not seeking their own gain, but to better others, they are concerned not only of their wellbeing but that of others. They give, for in giving they receive, they are authentic, true to themselves, and to others, they are bold and articulate themselves well, clearly, and firm. The noble possess a sense of purpose, they are pure and honest.

The Noble draw out change through love inspiration and encouraging the best in others, the small minded impose change by abuse and intimidation. The Noble creates opportunity for growth, the small minded is blind to ability of others, viewing him as a threat.

The Noble are deep rooted, seeking for the best in others, they are stable firm and forgiving, the small minded are shallow insecure and mean spirited. The Noble are joyful, without Fear, everything is possible to them, their lives, driven by love. The small minded are fearful, their lives is controlled by hate fear and limitation.

The Noble are grateful, they delight in life, and derive joy in it. The simple minded complain.

It's amazing how many people are hurt in our today's society. In my evaluation I believe Forty percent if not more of the world's population suffer from childhood traumas. In my interaction with many, I realised the root why the moral standards have decayed. One wonders why our world is going from bad to worse, it is due to undealt childhood traumas expressed in hateful outlets. The realisation brings me to the point of the requirement of the world's inner healing. Now more than ever, we require to start looking inwardly for the solutions to our world's problems. In my own experience of FGM, writing amongst other are the artistic expression that ignited a healing process in me, the process made it easier to understand the struggle around me and to find my place of representing restoration and fighting for human rights.

I am glad to have had good parents who have set a good example, that is before our family set fell apart, a common problem in the society, sadly my roots were disrupted when my family fell apart, then I experienced FGM. Many others, suffer similar experiences, but I am grateful to be given the channel to write, and share my life with others.

TRANSFORMING PAIN INTO POWER

Many in African countries are sadly victims of FGM. My aim in writing my book Fluegel fuer den Schmeterling, der Tag mein Leben began, is to encourage the victims of FGM to stand, reclaim their bodies, and fighting for their rights to be free of social and cultural oppressions.

In the book, I went back to my childhood when life was still intact, the influence of the good aspects of my Maasai Samburu culture, this was followed by a breakdown of the family which and then by FGM a negative factor in the culture.

Why do I want to confront the past?

The past contains our roots. In today's world we see the natural environment around us dwindling. Our spiritual environment is equally dwindling. It is our duty not just to fight for the conservation of the natural environment, but to look within ourselves and deal with the issues that bring about destruction of the spiritual environment of the human nature.

Join me in fighting against FGM, part of our human spiritual decay, affecting Africa, and fighting against other forms of abuse affecting Europe and the world. Together we can heal ourselves, together we could empower ourselves by fighting for the right to be free.

It's time for us lets stand up and fight!

We talk and discuss about global warming which is important but not about the decay of the moral standards in our communities. The introduction of spirituality will enable us to heal the state of moral decay which we face as a human race especially in the present times.

Human beings must learn to love with their hearts and not with their genitals the ability to do that will empower us to be much better people that are not self-centred but are given to creating a better world for everyone.

                Majesty and Glory to God.